Cookin' up the Blues

with

TABASCO®

brand pepper sauce

Contents

Marva Wright

Photo: © Michael P. Smith

When blues diva Marva Wright arrives, her presence can immediately captivate the smallest gathering to the largest concert audience. Yes, Marva is a big woman, but it is her foundation-shaking voice that demands respect. Sound carries a long way, and Marva seems capable of belting out numbers clean from her hometown of New Orleans to her many fans in Europe. Because her roots are in gospel—she didn't even begin singing blues until 1987, when she opened a show for Koko Taylor—Marva Wright's rapid ascent into the blues ranks sometimes seems unreal to her.

"I never dreamed of shaking hands and laughing with B.B. King and Charles Brown, or opening for Bobby 'Blue' Bland," Marva gushes. "Fats Domino even kissed me on my cheek and told me I was doing a good job!"

Rightfully so, because she's earned every honor bestowed upon her. "I got my experience working on Bourbon St. If you can make it on Bourbon, you can make it anywhere."

Her personal trials also played a major role in her transition from gospel to blues. "My father and mother were not married when I was born. He gave me his last name. I have brothers and sisters who don't own up to me. We all belonged to the same church, and they wouldn't even acknowledge me."

Marva channeled that pain into the title track of her second album, *Born With the Blues*. *Born With the Blues* is a stunning showcase of Marva's stratospheric vocals, complete with backing from a Louisiana dream band that includes Walter "Wolfman" Washington and Sonny Landreth on guitar. Domestic release of this gem should increase the lustre on Marva's rising star and have roots music aficionados swooning.

Like many great blues artists, Marva quietly downplays her darker hours and takes great relish in savoring the good times—and good food. Her church upbringing initiated a love affair with hearty stick-to-your-ribs fare. "There's a lot of cooking in church. We'd have suppers to raise money: fried chicken, potato salad, spaghetti and meatballs, green beans, chitlins, gumbo. A sister would have supper every Saturday."

She especially loves her red beans and rice, and likes to cook this dish for out-of-town visitors who haven't been exposed to the joys of New Orleans food.

"We had two people in recently, and they said they didn't want much to eat. Well, when they started eating, they couldn't get enough of it. This reserved woman just grabbed her bread and started dunking it in the gravy!"

So roll up your sleeves and start eating with reckless abandon; it'll do Marva's heart good.

Marva Wright's Red Beans & Brisket

Mesquite Smoked Brisket

3/4 cup red wine vinegar
1/2 cup packed brown sugar
1/2 cup unsweetened pineapple juice
1 (2-ounce) bottle TABASCO® brand pepper sauce (1/4 cup)
1/3 cup spicy mustard
1/3 cup molasses
3 tablespoons Worcestershire sauce
1 tablespoon chili powder
1 tablespoon minced onion
4-6 pound beef brisket

In a medium bowl combine all ingredients except brisket; mix well. Pour marinade over brisket; cover and marinate overnight.
Build a fire with mesquite or other good smoking wood on one side of a barbecue pit. When fire dies down to low, place brisket on other side of grill and cover grill. Cook over low heat for 6-8 hours or until brisket is tender, turning and basting with marinade occasionally.
(Use tongs to turn meat, rather than a meat fork, as juices will be lost if meat is pierced.)
Add additional wood to fire as needed.
When brisket is tender, remove from heat and let stand at least 15 minutes before slicing.
Serve warm.
Makes 16 to 20 servings.

Red Beans

1 pound of red beans, soaked in water overnight
2 whole onions, chopped
6 toes (cloves) of garlic
2 pounds of pickled tips (pickled pork or ham hocks can be substituted)
1 pound of chopped smoked sausage (optional)
1/2 pound (8 oz.) of hot sausage, whole (optional)
Salt & pepper to taste
2 tablespoons chopped fresh parsley
Dash TABASCO® brand pepper sauce
Hot cooked rice

Boil red beans, onion and garlic for 45 minutes. Meanwhile boil pickled tips until almost tender; drain water. Add pickled tips, smoked sausage and hot sausage to beans. Stir and continue to cook on medium fire until beans become creamy, stirring frequently. Add salt, pepper and parsley. Serve with hot rice and add TABASCO sauce to taste.

3

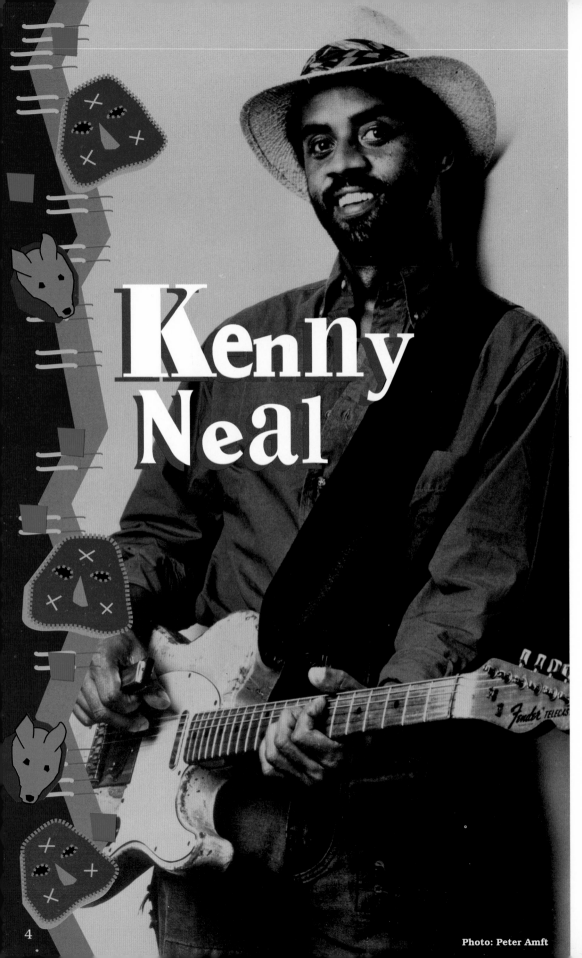

Kenny Neal

One of the things blues guitarist Kenny Neal makes sure to look for on his frequent trips around the world is African restaurants.

"They use a lot of the same spices and ingredients that we use in Louisiana," he explains. "Which makes sense because a lot of the Cajun and Creole foods and recipes originally came from Africa. 'Gumbo' and 'okra' are African words. If the African spices couldn't be found, French-Creole spices were substituted. It's all gone back and forth so many times that it's hard to say what recipes came first. All I know, it's all good."

Kenny Neal is heir apparent to the Delta blues crown. Though Kenny is firmly rooted in the deep blues he first learned from his father, Raful, he has coupled authenticity with a hard-edged, modern attack.

He grew up in Baton Rouge surrounded by a large, musical family. Along with his father, several of Kenny's brothers play music, and it's always a family affair when Kenny appears at the annual Jazz & Heritage Festival in New Orleans. Kenny joined Buddy Guy's band as a bassist at the age of 17 and learned much of his impassioned performance from the intense Guy. He has since matured and developed into a singular and outstanding guitar, harmonica and bass player; but his best instrument may just be his rich, raspy, highly expressive voice.

Expanding on his natural talent, in 1991 Kenny took New York City by storm as the star of Langston Hughes' play, *Mule Bone* (he also scored the play with Taj Mahal). He walked away with the Theatre World Award for "Most Outstanding New Talent On and Off Broadway."

Although he's known first and foremost as a blues musician, Kenny Neal also considers himself a pretty good cook. That's his mama's legacy to him.

"I got music in my blood from my daddy, but my mama taught me how to make gumbo. She makes the best. I'm trying to get her to write it down so we can get it in one of these cookbooks. I love cooking. I get in the kitchen and start sautéing some onion and green pepper and mushrooms, and then I just start throwing in whatever is in the fridge. Just smother it down and add some Tabasco sauce. I sprinkle it on everything. I love the stuff.

"I've become really good at tracking down the best soul food restaurants, no matter where I am. There's something about finishing a gig and finding the right restaurant where you can wind down, maybe have a couple of drinks to go with that spicy food, and just enjoy. I remember way back when I was just starting out, there was always a kitchen in the little barrooms we used to play—sometimes it was somebody's house—and after the gig we used to eat potato salad sandwiches. Two slices of white bread with fried chicken and potato salad. Man, it was great."

Kenny Neal's 'Dose & 'Dem Nuts

4 tablespoons butter or margarine, melted
2 teaspoons TABASCO® brand pepper sauce
1 teaspoon salt
2 cups raw, unsalted mixed nuts (such as pecans, walnuts, cashews, almonds, etc.)

Preheat oven to 300° F. In a small bowl combine butter, TABASCO sauce and salt. Mix well; pour over nuts and stir until well-coated. Spread nuts in a baking pan. Bake 20 minutes or until nuts are lightly toasted. Makes 2 cups.

Carol Fran   Clarence Hollimon

It was there that he and Carol hooked up for good in 1975. Since Black Top Records revived the duo's recording career in 1992 with *Soul Sensation*, Carol and Clarence have enjoyed a period of renewed success.

Besides his talent with spices, Carol says her husband is "a breakfast specialist." And, she admits, Clarence is also the more skilled with a frying pan. "He fries the best chicken in the house, I'm not ashamed to say. I can bake it or stew it, broil it or whatever else. But I'm not a good fry cook. He'll fry that chicken, and it's done all the way to the bone, 'cause he fries it slow. Now that's what kills me—that takes too much time! So when we have fried chicken, he fries it." Carol's forte is seafood—she can cook crawfish 21 different ways. And her gumbo, she maintains, is amazing. She and Clarence even make forays to the Texas Gulf Coast to secure fresh seafood right off the boats.

When blues and soul vocalist Carol Fran is asked whether her guitarist husband, Clarence Hollimon, is useful in the kitchen, her response is an immediate affirmative. "You know what he's good for? Cutting up the seasonings for me," she says. "He's very patient, and I'm always in a hurry. If the recipe calls for diced onions, I'll just chop 'em up. But he'll dice 'em."

Such teamwork parallels their relationship onstage, where the diminutive Clarence is generally a low-key figure in the background, providing the tasteful guitar platform from which the robust Carol serves up her potent vocal platters. "We do like a good dessert—we jell together," says Carol. Carol, a native of Lafayette, Louisiana, was 15 when she first hit the road with saxophonist Joe Lutcher's band. In the '60s, she was a regular at the Dew Drop Inn, New Orleans' famed R&B night spot, and scored a number of regional hits of her own.

Clarence backed legends Bobby "Blue" Bland, Little Junior Parker, Charles Brown and jazz singer Nancy Brown before heading back home to Houston to work as a session player for many years.

Carol says that she does her best cooking and singing when she's nervous. "For me, both of them are soothing. I'll do my best set if I'm nervous—I'll take the frustrations out on the music scene. And when I get nervous, I go to the kitchen and make some of the best meals trying to get away from whatever is bugging me. My favorite room in the house is the kitchen."

The food and music bond was forged when, as a young vocalist, Carol went on the road with the late bluesman Big Joe Turner.

"During crab season, if he rode in his limo from Galveston to Houston, there'd be crab claws all along the highway," says Carol, laughing at the memory. "He'd get in a room, and fifteen minutes later, you'd see the imaginary red light that said, 'Cook shop open.' Every time you'd walk in his room he was boiling a ham hock or frying a pork chop or cooking cabbage and pig tails."

That, says Carol, is where she picked up her habit of hotel room cooking. She likes to travel with an electric skillet, a small smokeless electric grill and a cache of utensils.

"Clarence doesn't like to eat out," explains Carol. "We'll have the only (hotel) room with pinto beans sizzlin'."

Carol Fran & Clarence Hollimon's Fried Chicken Salad

Fried Chicken Salad

Tarragon Dressing (recipe follows)
8 cups mixed salad greens, such as romaine, bibb,
   and leaf lettuce
1 cup torn radicchio or shredded red cabbage
1 cup shredded carrots
1 cup julienned zucchini
1 cup all-purpose flour
1 teaspoon salt
1/2 teaspoon black pepper
1/4 teaspoon garlic powder
1/2 cup buttermilk
1 tablespoon TABASCO® brand pepper sauce
1 pound boneless, skinless chicken,
   cut into 1/2-inch strips
Vegetable oil for deep-frying
4 small slices watermelon
1 tart green apple, sliced
Fresh tarragon sprigs

Prepare Tarragon Dressing and refrigerate
until ready to serve. In a salad bowl, combine
greens, radicchio, carrots and zucchini;
toss together and refrigerate.
In a bowl, combine flour, salt, pepper and garlic
powder; mix well and set aside. In another bowl,
combine buttermilk and TABASCO sauce; mix well
and set aside. Sprinkle chicken strips with additional
salt and pepper.
Heat oil to 375° F. Dip chicken in buttermilk mixture, then dredge in flour mixture. Fry in hot oil
about 2 minutes or until very crispy.
Drain on paper towels.
Arrange salad vegetables on plates and top with hot
chicken. Place slices of watermelon and apple on the
side and garnish with tarragon sprigs.
Serve with Tarragon Dressing. Makes 4 servings.

Tarragon Dressing

1 egg
1/2 cup vegetable oil
1/4 cup white wine vinegar
1 tablespoon fresh or dried tarragon
2 teaspoons spicy brown mustard
2 teaspoons TABASCO® brand pepper sauce
1/4 teaspoon salt

Blend egg in a food processor or blender until foamy.
With machine on, gradually add oil in a thin stream.
When mixture is thick and creamy, add remaining
ingredients and blend well. Makes 1 cup.

7

Lonnie BroOks

When Chicago bluesman Lonnie Brooks commands a bandstand, his wide-eyed looks following the sound of his booming voice and tenacious guitar solos, you get the impression he roams the woods and gobbles down a couple of medium-size critters for lunch every day.

That's kid stuff for Brooks, though. Literally.

Growing up in Dubuisson, Louisiana, Lonnie helped catch and prepare an assortment of local wildlife. He recalls, "I could cook anything. My daddy was a farmer, and my mother would stay with him and send me to the house around ten o'clock to cook lunch for the family. My grandfather was a trapper and a hunter and lived with us, so we ate a lot of pork and wild food: rabbits, coons, birds, squirrels. It's hard to kill a squirrel, 'cause they're so fast."

Luckily for the local animal contingent, Brooks dropped his hunting gear and kitchen utensils and picked up the guitar in his early twenties.

His talent was evident quickly, and he made a regional rock 'n' roll name for himself under the moniker "Guitar Junior," in addition to playing sideman to zydeco king Clifton Chenier and soul man extraordinaire Sam Cooke. In 1959, Brooks settled in Chicago, the nation's fiercely competitive and undisputed blues capital, where years of rough ghetto gigs eventually paid off for him with a contract with Alligator Records.

His first release for Alligator, *Bayou Lightning*, won the coveted "Grand Prix du Disque" from the 1980 Montreux Festival, initiating a string of solid albums that have been praised highly by everyone from *Rolling Stone* to *The New York Times*. After-hours compositions like "In the Dark" and "End of the Rope" showcase Lonnie's insightful songwriting, placing him in the company of contemporary masters such as B.B. King and Percy Mayfield.

Above all, the stage is Lonnie Brooks' bread and butter. He remains one of the hardest working men on the live circuit, averaging 250 nights a year. He has a cautious respect for life on the road—to maintain his intensity he exercises between shows. His teenage Daniel Boone diet has long been abandoned, and Lonnie now opts for more traditional fare.

"I have to put good food in my stomach," he says. "I was a vegetarian for five years, but my iron was low and my doctor told me to eat three pieces of meat a week. I love blackened fish, crawfish, gumbo, spicy food too. This chicken pot pie is real easy. I used to put 'em in the stove and bake 'em, eat 'em in the morning when I want something fast."

Lonnie Brooks'
Chicken Pot Pie

2 1/2 - 3 pound chicken
Water
1 stalk celery, chopped
1 onion, quartered
1 3-inch sprig fresh rosemary,
    or 1 teaspoon dried
1 tablespoon fresh thyme,
    or 1 teaspoon dried
1 1/4 teaspoons salt, divided
8 peppercorns
5 tablespoons butter or
    margarine, divided
1/3 cup all-purpose flour
1 cup half-and-half
1 teaspoon TABASCO®
    brand pepper sauce
1 cup sliced fresh mushrooms
1/2 cup cooked diced carrots
1/2 cup green peas
Pastry for a single-crust pie
1 egg yolk
1 tablespoon milk

Place chicken in a large pot and cover with water. Add celery, onion, rosemary, thyme, 1 teaspoon salt and peppercorns, and bring to a boil. Reduce heat and simmer 1 hour or until chicken is tender. Remove chicken from broth and discard skin and bones; cut chicken into bite-size pieces. Skim fat from broth and set aside 1 1/2 cups of the broth. (Use remaining broth in another recipe.)

Melt 4 tablespoons of the butter in a saucepan and stir in flour; mix well. Gradually stir in the 1 1/2 cups broth and the half-and-half. Cook and stir over medium heat until smooth and thickened; stir in TABASCO sauce and 1/4 teaspoon salt. In a skillet, sauté the mushrooms in the remaining butter until tender. Stir into white sauce along with carrots, peas and chicken.

Preheat oven to 450° F. Spoon mixture into a 10-inch pie plate and top with pastry, finishing edges as desired. Cut vents to allow steam to escape. Combine egg yolk and milk and brush lightly over pastry. Bake for 15 minutes. Reduce temperature to 350° F and bake 15 minutes longer or until crust is golden brown. Makes 6 servings.

9

Clarence "Gatemouth" Brown

Clarence "Gatemouth" Brown doesn't fiddle around—most of the time. But when the mighty Gate isn't playing his tasty guitar licks, stepping behind the drum kit, or picking a mandolin, the enigmatic bluesman breaks out his bow and dazzles with some serious sawin' on his fiddle.

"Country and Cajun and bluegrass are my real roots," he says, and simply shrugs off a straight blues label by "refusing to be put in a bag." Brown inherited his musical diversity from his father, who was a multi-instrument professional in a string band and started teaching his son shortly after Clarence was born in Louisiana in 1924. Gatemouth had an instinctual knack for absorbing a variety of styles, including jazz: "I'd listen to big band stuff—Count Basie, Duke Ellington. I liked Louis Jordan a lot, too, 'cause he was funny. I'm a positive person and don't like negative music."

Fellow musicians sense this, and Gate's upbeat energy and message have made him a highly respected session player. Along with his own illustrious career, recording for labels such as Duke/Peacock and Chicago's Alligator Records, Brown has found time to help out performers as varied as country's Roy Clark and current female chameleon Michelle Shocked.

His finest hour as a sideman came backing New Orleans piano legend and spiritual patriarch Professor Longhair. The two teamed up for Fess's *Rock 'n' Roll Gumbo*, often cited as one of the greatest albums of all time. Gatemouth makes the songs sound simple: "Fess said, 'they all that New Orleans style,' and I play what I think. A musician got to be a thinker."

Gate knows how to be creative in culinary adventures, too. He discovered his cornbread recipe "by accident. This cornbread recipe is an old one, and I thought it would taste good with some Tabasco butter. I like to put that on vegetables too."

Gate also makes cracklin' cornbread, which his mother used to do. "We knew that whatever we were doing, we would have a good dinner cooked when we got home." Not all of today's music impresses Gatemouth. "Some of the music today ain't got no feeling and does nothing for me. Some guys can play, and some can't. It's the same thing with food—some guys can do it, and some can't."

One taste of this honest recipe is proof that in the kitchen, as well as on stage, Clarence "Gatemouth" Brown doesn't play second fiddle to anyone.

Photo: Robert Barclay

Clarence "Gatemouth" Brown's Religious Corn Muffins

Corn Muffins

1 cup yellow cornmeal
1/2 cup all-purpose flour
3/4 teaspoon baking soda
1/2 teaspoon salt
1 cup buttermilk
1 egg
3 tablespoons bacon drippings or vegetable oil
1 teaspoon TABASCO® brand pepper sauce
1 tablespoon finely chopped red bell pepper
1 tablespoon finely chopped green bell pepper

Preheat oven to 450° F. Combine dry ingredients in a bowl. Stir together buttermilk, egg, bacon drippings and TABASCO sauce; add to dry ingredients and stir until just moistened. Stir in bell pepper. Grease 8 to 10 muffin cups and place in oven until hot. Remove muffin tin from oven and quickly fill muffin cups two-thirds full with batter and bake for 10 minutes or until golden brown.
Serve with TABASCO Butter Blend. Makes 8 to 10 muffins.

TABASCO® Butter Blend

1/2 cup butter, softened
2 teaspoons TABASCO® brand pepper sauce

Blend together in a small bowl. Serve with breads and on hot vegetables. Makes 1/2 cup.

11

The Memphis Horns

Wayne Jackson

Andrew Love

Photo Courtesy Memphis Horns

Over the years, Andrew Love and Wayne Jackson—known collectively as the Memphis Horns—have been one of the most sought-after horn sections in the business. They've brought added punch and soul to recordings by Otis Redding, Aretha Franklin, Al Green, Peter Gabriel and U2.

Those who record in the Horns' hometown of Memphis are often treated to an added bonus—genuine homecooked Southern meals, served up hot in the musicians' homes.

"We try to show them some Southern hospitality," says Wayne Jackson. "I think people always feel like they've been to a city when they've visited someone's home, rather than just staying in a hotel." Wayne—who plays trumpet—and Andrew—who handles saxophone—took the name of their signature dish from a session many years ago. "We did this King Curtis record, 'Memphis Soul Stew,' " remembers Wayne. "We started making a concoction that was kind of like a chili, and we just called it 'Memphis soul stew' for fun. There was hot sauce in there.

"I cooked this for all the bands we worked with. They come to my house. I can cook at studios [that have] a full kitchen. I cooked one time for a hundred people, and knocked 'em down on their knees, and they cried and begged for more.

"Last year I cooked for a bunch of Spanish guys, and a bunch of Japanese folks. And they all got Memphis Soul Stew, too. And they all loved it."

Andrew and Wayne have been partners since 1964 and have contributed to some 300 number one pop and R&B songs. They released their first album in 15 years, *Flame Out*, in 1992. While they may be a seamless brass section, their cooking duties are more segregated: Wayne handles chili-type dishes, while his partner specializes in barbecue.

"Andrew is the barbecue king," says Wayne.

"We do a helluva ribs," echoes Andrew. "Memphis is the rib capital of the world."

"One time the Robert Cray band was up here mixin' a record we had done in San Francisco," continues Wayne, "and Andrew and his wife did some ribs. The whole crowd went to Andrew's house, and almost nobody could leave. People just had to sit for two hours after they ate."

Both Wayne and Andrew grew up in Memphis, where "everybody's got one of them 55-gallon barrels cut in half in the back yard" for barbecuing. They've tried to export Memphis-style cooking around the world, but "it's kind of hard, 'cause you can't find the meat," says Wayne, although "you can carry a bottle of Tabasco with you."

"We like to cook," continues Andrew. "It might taste one way, then you have an idea to put something new in it, and try different things. It evolves, you know?"

They employ a similar approach in the studio: the Memphis Horns don't listen to rough versions of the songs they contribute to before entering the studio, preferring to walk in and let the feel and spontaneity of the moment create their parts on the spot.

"Our music and cooking are quite a bit alike when it comes to that," observes Wayne. "You can be inspired one day to do it one way, and the next you fall back and do your standard deal. There's no set recipe for what we do. You can go to new culinary heights."

The Memphis Horns' Soul Stew

1 tablespoon shortening
3 pounds chicken legs and thighs
3 cups chicken broth
1 ham hock
4 cups chopped tomatoes (with juice)
3 cups sliced fresh or frozen okra
2 cups fresh or frozen black-eyed peas
1 cup sliced carrots
3/4 cup pearl onions, peeled

1/2 cup chopped bell pepper
2 cloves garlic, pressed
4 teaspoons TABASCO® brand pepper sauce
1/2 teaspoon salt, or to taste
1/4 teaspoon dried oregano
1 bay leaf
1/2 cup all-purpose flour
3/4 cup water
Hot cooked rice

Melt shortening in a large Dutch oven or large deep casserole dish. Brown chicken, turning frequently. Add chicken broth, ham hock, vegetables, garlic, TABASCO sauce, salt, oregano and bay leaf. Cook 1 to 1 1/2 hours or until ham hock is tender. Remove chicken and ham hock and cool slightly; discard skin, bones and fat. Cut meat into bite-size pieces and return to stew.

In a small bowl, whisk flour and water, stirring well so there are no lumps. Slowly add mixture to stew, stirring constantly to prevent lumps. Cook until mixture boils, stirring often. Serve over rice. Makes about 6 servings.

BuckWheat ZydeCo

those on special occasions," recalls Buckwheat. "So I'd take some sewing thread and Mom would sneak a little piece of meat to me. And I'd go out to this little pond and catch crawfish. Mom would boil them and take the tails off and make a gravy out of it."

The family would also make ends meet by raising yard chickens and pigs. They'd go out on fishing trips, and young Buckwheat would spend afternoons in the woods, hunting rabbits with sticks.

Recently, it's been more difficult to find his favorite Louisiana food, says Buckwheat. As one of zydeco's most in-demand performers, he spends almost all of his time on tour. His solution? He travels with cooking supplies, including electric skillets and a deep-fryer.

"You don't find too much crawfish on the road," he says, "but you can have shrimp or etouffee. When I travel, I love checking out the culture and the food, but I always wind up going back to my own. So we just take Louisiana with us."

Buckwheat Zydeco's real name is Stanley Dural, but even his friends call him "Buck." Like many people, Buckwheat received his nickname in elementary school: his long, braided hair reminded his classmates of the "Little Rascals" character. He steeped his early music career in R&B and soul, until he was hired to play organ for the late "king" of zydeco, Clifton Chenier. Buckwheat went on to create his own signature blend of R&B, zydeco and rock, and his many recordings—including covers of songs by Bob Dylan and the Rolling Stones—have been compiled in a "best of" collection for Island Records.

It doesn't come as a surprise when Buckwheat admits that he's also been known to sing when he's cooking. "It's just you, the pot and the food," he says. "It just comes together, you know?"

Buckwheat also grew up with spicy food, he adds—note the four cloves of garlic in his Shrimp Creole. "Now with Tabasco," he says, "you got to respect it. Not enough is bad, and too much is bad. You got to know what you're doing."

At least that's what Buckwheat Zydeco learned from his mother. "She was a fantastic cook, man," he remembers.

There's always been a clear connection between food and music in Buckwheat Zydeco's life. As a child, his home was filled with both. "My mother used to sing to her food," he recalls. "She'd be over a stove singing spirituals, and when you'd smell all of that food coming out of that kitchen, man, you'd just say, 'Keep on singing, Mama!' " The Creole accordionist grew up in Lafayette, Louisiana, where he shared a two-room house with eleven brothers and sisters. Buckwheat was one of the oldest children, so he learned to cook from his mother—and he also helped bring some of the food to the table.

"We couldn't really afford shrimps—we'd just have

Buckwheat Zydeco's
Shrimp Creole

1/4 cup vegetable oil
1 medium onion, chopped
1 medium bell pepper, chopped
2 stalks celery, chopped
4 cloves garlic, minced
1 cup tomato sauce or canned,
  crushed tomatoes

1/2 cup water
1 tablespoon TABASCO® brand pepper sauce
Salt and pepper to taste
2 pounds shrimp, shelled and deveined
Hot cooked rice

In a skillet over medium heat, sauté onion, bell pepper, celery and garlic in oil until tender, about 10 minutes. Stir in tomato sauce, water, TABASCO sauce, salt and pepper, Heat to boiling. Reduce heat to low; cover and simmer 5 minutes. Add shrimp; cook 5 minutes or just until shrimp are cooked.
Serve over hot cooked rice. Makes 6 servings.

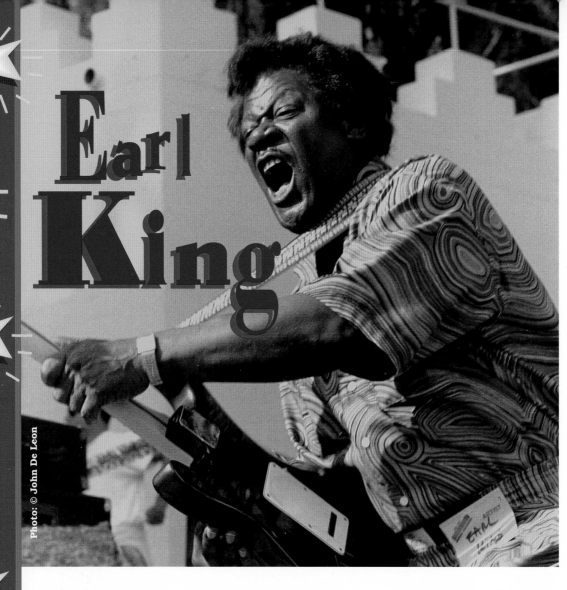

Earl King

Photo: © John De Leon

Mardi Gras anthems that are an integral part of the Carnival season. Recent recordings for Black Top Records, including the Grammy-nominated *Glazed*, *Sexual Telepathy* and *Hard River to Cross*, have introduced him to a new and appreciative generation, and he plans to keep on plugging away. "I don't know how old I'll get, but I'll still be writing songs," he states. "There's no end to that with me."

So it is with cooking. "I cook all the time. I'm in the kitchen all the time when I'm home. I'm just like Fats Domino."

He is "painstaking" when applying spices. "I've got to add my touch to something. Gumbo, that's a whole ball of wax. I've got one spice I put in gumbo, I don't tell what it is. It intermingles with the other spices and ingredients and brings out the other flavors."

The effort apparently pays off: Earl says that reviews of his specialties are always favorable. His oyster dressing? "I can't keep them away." His gumbo? "Nobody turns down my gumbo."

Earl King clearly remembers how—and why—he first found himself in the kitchen when he was just a lad. "My mom made me cook," Earl recalls. "She'd say, 'You'll be just like your daddy—he couldn't fry eggs. Come in here, boy.' "

In the long run, though, Earl was thankful for the lessons. "It paid off for me, 'cause I've been married a couple times, and neither one of my wives could cook. I'll see them sometimes, and they say, 'Earl, I still haven't gotten past that recipe you gave me.' "

Given Earl King's storytelling abilities, his magnificent head of hair, his risqué cartoons, and his tendency to drop out of sight for days on end whenever he decides he needs to, it is sometimes difficult to move beyond the image of King as character. But he is much more. Earl has been a mainstay on the New Orleans rhythm & blues scene since the 1950s, as both a songwriter and performer. The syncopated beat and lyrical twists in his music embody all the idiosyncracies that make the Big Easy's sound so distinctive. His songs have been covered by the likes of Robert Palmer ("Trick Bag"), the Neville Brothers, and Jimi Hendrix ("Come On"). His "Big Chief" is one of a handful of

Asked to choose between cooking and composing as his favorite creative activity, Earl names another. "My favorite is painting. To get away from things, a diversion, is to be painting. I get so frustrated when I can't find time to do that."

Given Earl's frequent tours abroad, he finds little time to paint and cook. So he must exercise his need to create onstage. "I tell everybody my greatest aspect of live performance is experimentation. Don't be afraid to make mistakes. Just use your imagination.

"Some people say, 'the blues, everybody's just rehashing things, that's the end of the line.' I say you can always add your own two cents. That's one of my greatest prizes—to work on a gig and to spontaneously come up with something I had no knowledge of. Some people will not try something they haven't practiced and practiced. Me, I do not care. BAM! Whatever pops into my head. That's my greatest asset. And sometimes it will surprise me, 'cause I don't know where it comes from."

"If somebody wanted the sum total of me, they could say, 'spontaneity.' "

Earl King's Burgoo

Earl King's Burgoo is a peppery stew similar to Brunswick stew made from a variety of meats and up to a dozen vegetables. It has long been a fixture at public barbecues in Kentucky, where huge iron pots simmer all day long over smoldering fires. Thus it has become known as Kentucky burgoo.

2 1/2 pound chicken, cut up
1 pound beef shank bones
1 pound lean beef or pork,
    cut into 1-inch cubes
1/2 pound lean lamb, cut into
    1-inch cubes
Water
1 large potato, peeled and diced
1 large onion, chopped
2 carrots, peeled and sliced
2 cups diced tomatoes
1 bell pepper, diced
1 cup sliced celery
1 cup lima beans
1 cup chopped cabbage
1 cup sliced okra
1 cup corn kernels, fresh
    or frozen
2 tablespoons vinegar or
    lemon juice
1 1/2 tablespoons TABASCO®
    brand pepper sauce
Salt and pepper to taste

In a large dutch oven or casserole dish, place chicken, beef shank bones, beef cubes, lamb cubes and enough water to cover. Reduce heat, cover and simmer at least 2 hours. Remove skin and bones and shred along with other meats. Skim fat from surface of broth; return chicken and all shredded meat to broth.

Add vegetables and remaining ingredients to pot and bring to a boil. Reduce heat and simmer at least 2 more hours, stirring occasionally and adding additional water if stew gets too thick. Makes about 1 gallon.

Elwood Blues

Dan Aykroyd

Catholic orphanage in Calumet City. From there he went to reform school and, later, Joliet.

"I learned to play harmonica in the orphanage, from a janitor named Curtis," remembered Elwood. "Because the stuff the nuns would give for supper would be clear soup and a hard roll—steam table food, you know, like that carrots, corn and peas mix. But me and Jake, we'd break away and we'd go down in the basement, and Curtis would cook up his own little special, like stuffed cabbage rolls, collard greens and black eye peas."

While on the lam, Elwood stocks his bluesmobile with the essentials: a frying pan, cooking oil, Tabasco sauce and ketchup. "I'm a real good grill chef when I put my mind to it," he said proudly. "I get some rocks together and make a little fire ring, and get some leaves and branches and twigs. Then I steal some vegetables. Sort of like hobo cooking, you know?

"One of my favorite things to do is 'All Day Potato,' " continued Elwood, pushing more change into the pay phone. "Basically, you start in the morning with a frying pan, put a little oil in it and some thinly sliced potatoes. And you just leave them in that low fire. You throw a little onion in there, lots of Tabasco sauce, and by the end of the day you have to scrape this hash off the bottom of the pan. It's really tasty, with all that carbon and crispiness.

"Now for dessert, you go to a coffee shop or bakery and you get a plain doughnut—no glazing or nothing—and you soak that in oil, and you just put that on a grill, and you just grill that doughnut up." Elwood paused. "Grilled doughnuts. Yeah, grilled doughnuts."

The Elwood sandwich can be found on the menu at the House of Blues clubs in Cambridge, New Orleans and Los Angeles, all of which are co-owned by Elwood's close friend, actor Dan Aykroyd. The Blues Brothers Band is currently on a world tour, featuring Eddie Floyd on lead vocals. If he's able to elude the law, Elwood joins the band for House of Blues openings.

But Elwood rarely gets the opportunity to prepare the sandwich that bears his name. "Of course, getting a chicken is a big thing," he admitted. "If I can't catch it, I ain't eating it."

The Elwood Sandwich, like everything that Elwood Blues cooks, is road food. More accurately, it's side-of-the-road food—or side-of-the-railroad-track food.

Elwood Blues, you see, is on the run. He's served time in Joliet Prison in Illinois for Grand Theft Auto and Grand Theft Bus, and he doesn't want to go back. "I've got a routine worked out," he explained, speaking from a pay phone in an undisclosed location. "I move into town and I call up a rental agency, and I rent a TV, a couch and a chair. I stay about three months until they come to repossess, and I take the TV with me and I move on to another town. There I sell the TV and put the money down on the next rental."

With his brother, the late Jake Blues, Elwood made several legendary appearances in the 1970s on "Saturday Night Live," which led to a Blues Brothers movie and record deal. But the lanky harp player with the trademark sunglasses and the handcuffed briefcase had a humble beginning: he was born in the back seat of a car near a steel mill in Hammond, Indiana. Then Elwood was taken from his parents and placed in a

Elwood Blues'

Chicken Sandwich

Chicken Sandwich

1 (6-ounce) boneless, skinless chicken breast
Louisiana Spice Mix (recipe follows)
1 tablespoon butter or margarine
1 onion roll, split and toasted
Chili-Garlic Mayonnaise (recipe follows)
1 leaf lettuce
1 large slice tomato
2 tablespoons sour cream
Pickled jalapeño slices
TABASCO® brand pepper sauce

Sprinkle chicken breast generously with spice mix. In a small skillet, melt butter over medium-high heat and add chicken. Cook about 3 minutes on each side or until nicely browned.
Spread roll with Chili-Garlic Mayonnaise on each side.

Place chicken on bottom half of roll; top with lettuce, tomato, sour cream, jalapeño, and TABASCO sauce and then top half of roll. Makes 1 serving.

Louisiana Spice Mix

2 1/2 tablespoons salt
2 1/2 tablespoons paprika
2 tablespoons garlic powder
1 1/2 tablespoons onion powder
1 tablespoon cayenne pepper
1 tablespoon dried oregano
1 tablespoon dried thyme
2 teaspoons coarse black pepper
1 1/2 teaspoons white pepper

Combine all ingredients in a jar and shake till well mixed. Makes about 1 cup.

Chili-Garlic Mayonnaise

1 cup mayonnaise
1 tablespoon chili garlic paste (see note)
1/2 teaspoon Jamaican jerk seasoning (see note)
3 large cloves garlic, pressed

Combine all ingredients in a small bowl and mix well. Makes 1 cup.

Note: Chili garlic paste is available in Oriental food shops and other food specialty stores. Jamaican jerk seasoning is also available in food specialty stores, but if you can't find it, try the following mixture: 1 teaspoon ground allspice, 1 teaspoon ground thyme, 1 teaspoon garlic powder, 1 teaspoon sugar, 1/2 teaspoon cayenne pepper, 1/2 teaspoon black pepper, 1/2 teaspoon ground nutmeg, and 1/2 teaspoon ground cinnamon.

Tinsley Ellis

Rising blues rock guitar singer Tinsley Ellis had little say in whether or not he liked grits. "Being a son of the South, it's food that I've eaten all my life...grits especially," says Tinsley, who grew up in Florida and Georgia and currently resides in Atlanta.

His mother used to cook a lot of grits, and Tinsley carries on the tradition. "It's easy, too," he promises.

Which is convenient, as most of his time is spent with his guitar. Tinsley's life work as a bluesman was determined at age 14 when, while seated in the front row of a B.B. King concert in Miami Beach, the young Ellis was handed a broken string by the great King. Thus inspired, he went on to play with blues-rock bands on the southeastern circuit before making his solo debut in 1988 with *Georgia Blue* (on Alligator Records). Subsequent solo releases have seen Tinsley expanding his creative role by writing, arranging and contributing to the production, as well as laying down fiery guitar licks. Tinsley seems determined to earn his kudos the old-fashioned way: by hitting the road, and hard. The tour for *Trouble Time* (1992) brought him to 44 states, as well as Europe and Canada. That tour nearly provided an inspirational moment on a par with the B.B. King experience, when Jimi Hendrix' father stopped by a show in Seattle.

"He came out and invited me to play Jimi's guitars," says Tinsley. "Unfortunately, I had to leave town. But I really want to do that next time I get back. I sure do want to play them. They're all left-handed guitars, but I'd still give it a try."

Although Tinsley misses the cooking of the South when he's away, he is not averse to exploring the dining possibilities offered by other regions.

"You know, every part of America—and really every part of the world—has got its own food. My favorite food is in the South, particularly the Gulf Coast."

"But then you get a great breakfast in the Midwest—they've got their pork products down. And up in the Northeast is where you're going to get your really good pizza and your good delicatessen kinds of food. And, of course, the Southwest with the spicy food down there. Every part of the country has really got its thing."

Photo: Peter Kerez

The only problem is that certain Southern staples—namely grits—aren't available elsewhere in the country.

"We can't get grits north of Virginia, and west of Missouri is a toss-up as to whether you're going to get grits or not. I've got some guys in my band who are from the South, but I've got some guys that can't stand grits. Grits are a matter of personal taste— and I don't have 'em every day. Grits are best when they're dressed up, and garlic cheese is my favorite dress-up for a grit."

He'll cook grits at home, along with other simple Southern fare and the occasional stir fry, but he doesn't consider himself much of a chef. "I'm a consumer," he says. "If you're gone as much as I am, you're a consumer, almost exclusively."

Grilliades &True Grits

Tinsley Ellis'

Grilliades

Brown Roux (recipe follows)
2 pounds veal or beef round steak
Salt and black pepper
1/4 cup olive oil
3/4 cup chopped bell pepper
1/2 cup chopped onion
1 stalk celery, chopped
2 large cloves garlic, minced
1 1/2 cups chopped tomatoes
1 1/2 cups beef broth
1/2 cup red wine
1 tablespoon TABASCO® brand pepper sauce
2 bay leaves
1 teaspoon fresh thyme, or 1/4 teaspoon dried
1 cup sliced fresh mushrooms (optional)
2 tablespoons chopped fresh parsley
Garlic Cheese Grits (recipe follows)

Prepare Brown Roux and set aside. Pound veal to 1/4-inch thickness and cut into serving-size pieces; sprinkle with salt and pepper.
Heat olive oil in a large heavy skillet over medium-high heat; brown meat, about 3 to 5 minutes per side. Remove from skillet and set aside.
Add bell pepper, onion, celery, and garlic to skillet; cook 5 minutes, stirring occasionally. Add roux, tomatoes, broth, wine, TABASCO sauce, bay leaves, thyme, and salt and pepper to taste; stir until roux is dissolved. Bring mixture to a boil; reduce heat and add meat and, if desired, mushrooms. Cover and cook 1 hour or until meat is tender, stirring occasionally and adding additional broth or water if gravy gets too thick. Stir in parsley and serve with Garlic Cheese Grits. Makes 6 servings.

Brown Roux

1/4 cup all-purpose flour
1/4 cup vegetable oil

Combine flour and oil in a small heavy skillet over medium-high heat. Cook and stir until roux is dark brown (the color of a dirty copper penny), about 15 minutes. Remove from heat and continue stirring a few minutes until roux cools enough to stop cooking. Makes about 1/3 cup.

Garlic Cheese Grits

3 cups water
3/4 cup quick (not instant) yellow grits
1/4 cup butter or margarine
1 1/2 cups shredded sharp cheddar cheese
1 clove garlic, pressed
1 teaspoon TABASCO® brand pepper sauce
1/2 teaspoon salt
1 egg, beaten

Preheat oven to 350° F. Bring water to a boil in a saucepan; stir in grits and cook according to package directions. Remove from heat and stir in butter, cheese, garlic, TABASCO sauce and salt, mixing well. Stir a spoonful of the grits mixture into egg, then add egg mixture to remaining grits; mix well. Spoon into a buttered 1 quart casserole and bake for 45 minutes.
Makes 6 servings.

21

Lynn August

Photo: © 1993 Rick Olivier

and margarine for the butter. Then use low-fat cheese. It tastes just as good, he promises. (Lynn adds that his favorite trick is to serve sugar-free desserts to his friends—without telling them what it is.)

If anyone can convert Creole cooking into health food, it's Lynn August. Throughout his musical career, Lynn has been one of zydeco's most versatile performers. Born into a French-speaking family, when Lynn turned 11 he began playing drums for the flamboyant bandleader Esquerita (an early teacher of Little Richard).

He moved on to a solo career playing keyboards in area hotels and restaurants, where his repertoire consisted of blues and R&B. After a stint as sideman to zydeco musician Marcel Dugas, Lynn picked up his own accordion. In the late 1980s, he formed his band, The Hot August Knights.

A bluesy vocalist and polished piano-key accordion player, Lynn is a fixture on Louisiana stages as well as at festivals around the world. He continues to incorporate diverse styles into his music, and has recorded everything from Fats Domino tunes to old Creole spirituals.

On a recent release for Black Top Records, Lynn's eclectic approach was augmented by legendary New Orleans R&B guitarist Snooks Eaglin.

But there's one thing that Lynn isn't flexible about: spicy food. He has to have it. He even named one of his albums *Sauce Piquante*, after a popular Creole dish. There was one tour stop, he remembers, where a host prepared a pot roast for the band. "But it wasn't seasoned," he recalls. "Then they started saying how we think we can cook better, just because we're from Louisiana. So the next day, they prepared another dish for us, and they said, 'Man, we really got it hot for you now.' But we could hardly taste it."

"Creole food is more than just hot—it has garlic, onions, celery. But we're still used to that spice—it's what we grew up on. In fact, when we used to go abroad, we used to pack a bottle of Tabasco sauce, just in case. But now most places we go to already have it."

When zydeco musician Lynn August was diagnosed as diabetic, he knew he would have to change the way he prepared his favorite foods. Because, says Lynn, growing up in a Creole community in Lafayette, Louisiana, didn't exactly prepare him for a life of low-fat cooking.

"I remember in the summer when my grandfather and his neighbors used to make what they called a *boucherie*," he explains. "They didn't have storing facilities for meat, so one person would supply the hog or the calf, and we'd all share. Then the next week, somebody else would have it. I remember eating cracklin' (deep-fried pieces of fat) right out of the pot—I tell you what, I wouldn't dare try that now."

Instead, the popular accordionist—along with his wife, Pat, and his son, Lynn Jr.—has created new versions of his favorite Creole dishes. For example, Lynn Jr. bakes cakes and pies without sugar. And they eat a lot of vegetables—a recent autumn week found Lynn and his wife canning seven bushels of okra and 30 dozen ears of corn.

If you want to prepare shrimp or crawfish fettuccine his way, says Lynn, just substitute yogurt for the half-and-half,

Lynn August's Crawfish Fettuccine

1 pound fettuccine noodles
3/4 cup butter or margarine (1 1/2 sticks)
2 medium onions, chopped
2 stalks celery, chopped
1 bell pepper, chopped
4 green onions, chopped
1 tablespoon all-purpose flour
1 1/2 pounds peeled crawfish tails (or shrimp)
2 tablespoons chopped fresh parsley
1 cup half-and-half

1 (8-ounce) box pasteurized processed cheese,
   cut into 1-inch cubes
3 cloves garlic, minced
1 tablespooon TABASCO® brand pepper sauce
1/4 cup grated Parmesan cheese
Salt and pepper to taste

Cook fettuccine according to package directions; drain and set aside. Meanwhile, in a large saucepan over medium heat, melt butter. Add onions, celery, bell pepper and green onions; cooking until tender, about 10 minutes; stir occasionally. Stir in flour, mixing well. Add crawfish (or shrimp) and parsley, simmer 5 minutes. Add half-and-half, cheese, garlic and TABASCO sauce. Bring almost to a simmer, then reduce heat to low and cook 5 minutes. Do not let boil. Toss mixture with cooked fettuccine; top mixture with Parmesan cheese; salt and pepper to taste. Makes 8 servings.

23

Photo: Henry Diltz

The always-amusing Joe Walsh thinks he first encountered his rather offbeat tuna casserole recipe while attending Kent State University in the late 1960s.

"It's an old recipe from college," says the guitarist. "I don't know who showed it to me. Probably my first wife...no, I cooked it for her. I dunno. If you've got 37 cents, it was a full meal, at least in those days. It holds up in court—it's good stuff. It's about the closest thing to meat and potatoes with fish."

If you double the ingredients, Joe notes, you can serve twice as many people. "That will fill you up, and you won't have nightmares."

He admits that he is no wizard in the kitchen. "I'm getting into a wok a lot lately. I really don't have what you need to cook a Thanksgiving Day turkey. What I do is nibble on it while it's cooking. By dinner, I'm full, and I don't want anything to do with it. I recommend a wok. Or go out to dinner."

Joe Walsh's prolific recording career has encompassed (so far) four albums with the early-'70s power trio The James Gang, three as a member of the Eagles, and ten solo projects. As a member of the Eagles, the seminal California country-rock outfit of the '70s, Walsh co-wrote "Life In the Fast Lane." Later, he scored a hit single as a solo artist with "Life's Been Good," a sarcastic look at rock star excess. Along the way, he also ran (unsuccessfully) for President in 1980.

Walsh was a relative late-comer to the blues. In high school, he says he was "too busy practicing oboe" to fiddle with the guitar. Later, while at Kent State, "I was learning Clapton licks—I didn't want to learn from the guys he learned from. I didn't study them. I studied the English school."

Once he had been introduced to the blues, Joe quickly made up for lost time. He befriended the late great Albert King, after Joe and King's manager opened a recording studio together. "What was wonderful was I had studied him," says Joe of King. "He was the one guy I studied.

"I used to call him Pop, and he called me Son. He used to call me 'Joseph.' 'Joseph, why you got to make all them faces when you play guitar? Why can't you stand still? I saw you on TV, and I had to change the channel.'

"Albert could [care less] about the Eagles. He would fire on [yell] at me: 'Son, come over here!' "

Not only did Albert not care for Joe's onstage antics, but he also wasn't too keen about Walsh's Tuna Casserole. "He hated tuna fish casserole," remembers Joe. "You know what Albert King liked? Fried chicken."

Albert would often regale Walsh with tales about the old days. In return, Joe helped assemble the band that played on King's last record. They spent much time jamming (Joe says he played "intelligent rhythm" to King's lead). Walsh played "Amazing Grace" on slide guitar at King's funeral in Memphis. His final message to his friend? " 'So long, Pop.' And I didn't make any funny faces."

And although Joe counts a host of blues greats among his acquaintances—including B.B. King, Etta James and Freddie King—Albert King will always occupy a special place in his heart. "With all due respect to all the Kings, Albert was special. It was an honor and a privilege to play with him."

Joe Walsh's All-American Tuna Fish Casserole

Get this —

- 2 of those cat food sized cans of tuna fish (The kind packed in water, not oil)
- A bag of those seashell-shaped noodles (16-oz. bag)
- A can of peas
- 2 cans of "golden" mushroom soup
- An 8-pack of American cheese slices
- 2 teaspoons TABASCO® brand pepper sauce

Turn on your oven to +/- 350° F. Get a big pot. Put lots of water, a big spoonful of salt, and just a little bit of cooking oil in it (so just a couple of bubbles of it float around on top of the water). Make it boil. Keep it that way...no lid. When it's boiling, dump in the noodles, stir them around every chance you get. I don't know how long; for example, altitude is a factor (high altitude pasta takes longer to prepare than sea-level pasta). Make sure to keep it boiling!

While you are doing that... get a big bowl. Put the "golden" mushroom soup, the peas and the tuna fish (minus the water in the cans they come in) and TABASCO sauce in the bowl. Mix it up so it's all gooshy and the peas are evenly distributed. Every now and then, eat one of the noodles. When they chew like gum, drain all the water out, put some butter in there, and stir it all around until it melts all over the noodles.

Dump the noodles into one of those Pyrex cooking things, dump the tuna fish goosh on top, spread it evenly, and put that in your oven for +/- 25 minutes or so. Stir the whole mess up after 15 minutes. No lid. When it's bubbling like a toxic waste site, layer the cheese on top (4-5 slices) and put whatever that is back in the oven until the cheese is more than melted but less than burnt. It will be very hot! Now carefully take it out of the oven.

Go tell everybody it's time to eat. I recommend a couple big old ice cream scoops of it — in a big bowl or on a plate, a tossed salad, and bread and butter.

Like spaghetti, for some reason, it tastes extra special the next day when you heat it back up — either for breakfast or at halftime.

Enjoy. Joe Walsh

Photo: Sandro Miller

Koko Taylor

1984 she won the coveted Grammy for "Best Blues Recording." She has also won the blues community's highest honor, the W.C. Handy Award, a dozen times. With appearances on television and a cameo in the David Lynch film *Wild at Heart*, Koko is probably the most recognized and in-demand woman blues singer of all time. Not bad for a lady who started working in the cotton fields near Memphis when she was six years old.

Koko Taylor moved to Chicago in the early '50s and started sitting in with her favorite bands, performing a song or two for a few bucks or just for fun. One night in 1964, while singing with Howlin' Wolf, she was discovered by Willie Dixon, who was so impressed by the young Koko that he hustled her into the studio and produced her first album. One of the tunes included in that effort was the Dixon-penned "Wang Dang Doodle."

"I thought it was the silliest sounding song I ever heard talk of," Koko says. It became a million seller. Koko now belongs to the Alligator Records family.

With a touring schedule that includes some 200 dates a year, Ms. Taylor is not always able to stick to her preferred diet. "It's hard to eat what you're supposed to eat when you're on the road. I love spicy foods and like Tabasco sauce a whole lot. It's good for seasoning and I use it on the table to sprinkle on food...it's real tasty."

Life on the road can also be boring, and one thing a hard-working blues shouter like Koko is always looking for is a good place to eat.

"Food relates to blues because they're both good for your body and good for your soul. Blues music is healing, it's therapy. It revives people who listen to it. My music is designed to make people pep up, look up, feel good about themselves. It gives them something to think about tomorrow...a special song I did that they like, or the good time they had. Good food will do the same thing. We all have to eat certain food that is healing to the body.

"So the music and food go right together."

When you're the "hardest-working lady in show business"—in addition to being the "Queen of the Blues"—that doesn't leave a lot of time for the kitchen. Koko Taylor, who has earned both of these titles, wishes she had more time at the stove.

"I love to cook," she says. "This jambalaya recipe is one of my favorites. I think I'm a pretty good cook, and I love to cook New Orleans specialties like red beans and rice or gumbo. I can make some of the best New Orleans gumbo in Chicago you most ever tasted. I'll tell you who learned me how to make the gumbo—(the late blues songwriter extraordinaire and record exec) Willie Dixon's wife, Marie. She's from New Orleans and she learned me how to make it with okra and corn and this and that. Mmmmm mmmmm."

In the tough, male-dominated blues world, Ms. Taylor has earned every important laurel, award and kudo that there is. In

Koko Taylor's

Jivin' Jambalaya

1 cup white rice (long grain)
1 cup wild rice
Boiling water
1 pound fresh medium-size shrimp
3 boneless, skinless chicken breasts
1/4 cup butter or margarine
1/2 cup chopped onion
1/3 cup chopped celery
1/3 cup chopped red bell pepper
1/3 cup chopped green bell pepper

2 cups chicken broth
1/2 teaspoon salt
1/2 teaspoon black pepper
2 teaspoons TABASCO® brand pepper sauce
2 tablespoons chopped parsley

Cook white rice according to package directions and set aside. Cook wild rice according to package directions and set aside.

Cook shrimp in boiling water for 2 to 3 minutes; peel and devein, set aside. Cook chicken in boiling water 5 minutes or until done; dice meat and set aside. Melt butter in a large skillet over medium heat. Add onion, celery, and bell pepper and cook until tender, about 10 minutes. Add broth, salt, pepper, shrimp, and chicken and bring to a boil; stir in rice. Reduce heat and simmer until broth is absorbed, about 20 minutes. Stir in TABASCO sauce. Sprinkle with parsley and serve. Makes 8 servings.

27

Photo: Frederick Toma

The Thomas Family

With the possible exception of soul music, the hottest topic in Rufus and Lorene Thomas' house has to be soul food.

In the middle of a Saturday afternoon conversation with his wife, Rufus Thomas gets things rolling when he proclaims that "we are lovers of lunch meat."

"*He* is a lover of lunch meat," corrects Lorene.

"Lorene doesn't eat chitlings."

"Anybody can have them if they want," says Lorene, showing diplomacy.

"You eat everything about a hog—there's nothing about a hog that you don't use. You know that?"

"That sounds terrible."

"Now that doesn't sound bad!" protests Rufus. "That's pig feet, the tail, and when you call yourself 'eating high off the hog,' that's the best part of it. And during the New Year, you have black-eyed peas and hog head. That's for good luck."

"No, I don't like hog head."

When asked about his own cooking, Rufus Thomas says that he is "the best—"

"Eater!" interrupts Lorene, laughing.

Yes, agrees Marvell Thomas, the oldest of the three Thomas children, everyone can have their own opinions about food—but his was a one-cook home.

"If my mother decided we were having meat loaf every Thursday, we had meat loaf every Thursday," he explains. "Obviously, she had total autonomy in the kitchen."

Lorene Thomas isn't the famous member of this Memphis musical dynasty—it was father Rufus Thomas and daughter Carla who cut some of the biggest hits for the celebrated Memphis soul label called Stax. (The Thomas' recordings are included in two boxed sets on the Atlantic and Fantasy labels.) Marvell played keyboards for Stax and now runs "Sweet Chariot Enterprises," a Memphis music production company. Youngest daughter Vaneese is a commercial jingle singer in New York, and can be heard as an Uh-Huh® girl on Ray Charles' Pepsi® commercials.

But considering the high level of activity in the Thomas house, says Marvell, dinnertime was critical: "It was really the only time when we were all together, sharing stories of the day."

After the Top 10 successes of such songs as Carla's "Gee Whiz" and Rufus' "Walking the Dog," these shared meals became rarer. Touring schedules took Rufus into strange lands with people who didn't know about grits and cornbread.

"And anytime you can't cook a pan of cornbread," says Rufus, "man, you're out of it."

Along with the South Memphis Soul Loaf (named by Marvell), a typical Thursday table would contain mashed potatoes, gravy made from the loaf drippings, cornbread, salad, greens and some kind of beans. "And dessert," adds Lorene. "That's what soul food means—always something sweet at the end." That end-of-the-meal payoff might be lemon icebox pie, sweet potato pie, coconut cake or brownies.

Marvell remembers watching his mother in the kitchen, putting odds and ends into a pot and turning it into something wonderful. "For once we have to take second fiddle to what my mother has done," he concludes. "She was the glue that held all of us creative musical types together."

The Thomas Family's South Memphis Soul Loaf

Soul Loaf

Topping (recipe follows)
3 pounds lean ground chuck
3 eggs, beaten
1 large onion, finely chopped
1 large bell pepper, finely chopped
1/4 cup finely chopped celery
1 large clove garlic, minced
2 tablespoons TABASCO® brand pepper sauce
25 unsalted wheat crackers, finely crumbled
1 teaspoon coarsely ground black pepper
1 teaspoon ground cumin
1/4 teaspoon salt, or to taste (optional)
1/2 cup sliced fresh mushrooms

Prepare Topping and set aside.
In a large bowl combine ground chuck, eggs, onion, bell pepper, celery, garlic, and TABASCO sauce; set aside.
In a small bowl combine cracker crumbs, pepper, cumin and salt; mix well. Add to ground meat mixture, mix with hands until well blended.

Preheat oven to 350° F. Spray 2 loaf pans with cooking spray and press mixture into pans. Spread half of the topping on each loaf and top each with half of the mushrooms. Cover pans with aluminum foil. Bake for 1 hour.

Cool 15 minutes and turn out onto serving platter. Serve hot, or chill and cut into 1-inch slices for sandwiches. Makes about 12 servings.

Topping

1 (8-ounce) can tomato sauce
2 tablespoons cooking sherry
1 tablespoon Italian seasoning
1 teaspoon TABASCO® brand pepper sauce

Combine all ingredients in a small bowl and mix well. Makes 1 1/4 cups.

AerOsmith

Over the years, Aerosmith guitarist Joe Perry has been an unofficial ambassador for two of his consuming passions: the blues and hot sauce.

The blues grabbed Joe early on. Like many American rockers who came of age in the late 1960s and early 1970s, Perry was first exposed via the British rock bands he listened to as a kid (those bands also brought along blues artists like Buddy Guy and B.B. King as opening acts). Before they could drive, Perry and his pals would take the bus into Boston from their homes in nearby Hopedale to catch blues acts. Later, while attending prep school, he traded blues records with class-mates.

His earliest bands were blues-based, and from there it was a short leap to the bluesy hard rock that became Aerosmith's stock-in-trade. Marked by Perry's lead guitar work and vocalist Steven Tyler's rasp, the Aerosmith sound has endured for 17 albums over 20-plus years. After temporarily disbanding in the early '80s, the original members regrouped and launched a creative and commercial resurgence with 1987's *Permanent Vacation* that is still going strong, making Aerosmith one of the most successful American rock bands of all time.

The Aero-catalog boasts several obvious paeans to the blues, most notably the classic "Reefer Head Woman," and "Hangman's Jury," off of *Permanent Vacation*. (In keeping with the band's scholarly interest in the subject, Perry says the group traced the history of a vocal effect they used on "Hangman's Jury" all the way back to an old Leadbelly recording.)

Perry distinctly recalls the first time he heard Freddie King's classic blues recording of "Goin' Down" and the profound effect it had on him. "I must have been about 17 or 18," remembers Perry, "and I was driving my car and it came on the radio. I had to pull over."

Perry now has a chance to return the favor: toward the end of Aerosmith sets, he generally takes over the vocal chores from Steven Tyler and accompanies himself on lead for "Goin' Down," "Red House," or some other blues standard, thereby introducing the material to the thousands of kids who turn up when Aerosmith comes to town. Perry says he appreciates the fact that he might be exposing the blues to legions of new fans, but he has his own reasons for including the selections: "I do it because I get off on it."

And, just like he was taken in by the blues' spell years ago, he marvels at the ease with which audiences take to blues standards that they may be unfamiliar with. "In every town we play, people come up to me after the show to tell me how much they liked them."

Perry's worldwide travels with Aerosmith have made it easier for him to indulge one of his hobbies: in keeping with his status as a major fan of spicy foods, for years he has collected hot sauces from around the globe. Perry says he favors those from Louisiana and the Caribbean. Tabasco sauce, he notes, is a staple.

Just as he brings blues to the masses, Perry lobbies his fellow rockers on the joys of hot sauce: he once sent a box of choice sauce selections to the English farm of Led Zeppelin guitarist (and fellow hot sauce connoisseur) Jimmy Page.

For the Boston-based dish in this recipe, Perry prefers scrod, a type of cod native to New England waters, but says that any whitefish will do. And though he is the closest thing to a blues-man in his family, he admits that his wife is the real cook when it comes to scrod: "Her version always comes out better than mine."

Aerosmith's Scrod with Onions

Scrod is a young cod or haddock, especially one that has been split and made ready for cooking.

Canola oil or vegetable cooking spray
1 very large Spanish or Vidalia onion, chopped
1 tablespoon soy sauce, divided
TABASCO® brand pepper sauce, to taste
2 tablespoons water
1 pound scrod filets

Lightly coat a large skillet with canola oil or cooking spray.
Place over medium-high heat and add the onion, half of the soy sauce, and a couple of dashes of TABASCO sauce. Cover and cook 2 minutes, stirring occasionally.
Add the water and scrod. Sprinkle with remaining soy sauce and a couple more dashes TABASCO sauce. Cover and simmer, occasionally spooning onion mixture over filets, until fish flakes easily, about 5-10 minutes.
Serve on a large fish platter with additional TABASCO sauce, if desired.
Makes 4 servings.

Photo: ©Brian Ashley White

Terrance Simien

Cooking, then, was not just the domain of the women of the community. "Men would do it, but they wouldn't do it in the kitchens in their houses—they'd make too much of a mess," says Terrance. "They'd build these outdoor kitchens. They had an old house or old camper where they'd all get together and make a mess. The next morning, they'd have to clean it up."

An offer of free food and beer was usually enough to ensure that a couple of musicians were on hand to provide live entertainment. "That's how they'd get some of the musicians to show up—free food and beer," laughs Simien. "They'd come runnin'."

Young Terrance felt privileged to be included in this men's ritual. "It was a cool thing to hang out with the older men of the community. You'd hear all kinds of stories—as the beers would go down, the stories would get longer and longer and more interesting."

As Simien's reputation as an accordionist began to spread, he found that the number of invitations he received increased, but with a catch: "I used to get invited to a lot of these gatherings, from all over the place—one thing I had to do was bring my accordion."

His talents, polished at *sauce piquantes*, soon brought him acclaim outside of Acadiana. Simien was not yet 20 years old when he and his Mallet Playboys broke out of southwest Louisiana in the mid-'80s with a hard-charging, headbanging brand of zydeco. His performances are energetic, sweaty affairs that generally fill the dancefloors.

Now that he spends some 200 nights on the road annually, he is unable to attend as many *sauce piquantes*. "They don't do it as often as they used to, and I always miss them whenever they do have one," he laments.

His own cooking dates back to his childhood. Terrance and his siblings had to contribute to cooking chores after their mother developed crippling arthritis. After Terrance's sister married and his brother went off to college, that left the future musician to cover much of the food preparation. "It was just basic stuff. Meat and rice, stuff like that."

Nowadays, he cooks around his home in Lafayette a bit, usually dishes indigenous to southwest Louisiana—crawfish etouffee, gumbo. "I can cook just about anything that I was brought up on."

Growing up in the small southwest Louisiana town of Mallet, soul and zydeco crooner Terrance Simien recalls the link between food and music being established early on at gatherings called *sauce piquantes*—cookouts held by the men of the community.

"It was mainly a social gathering, people talking about each other in the community, a little gossiping going on, a little storytelling about how times were so hard years back," remembers Terrance.

The gathering took its name from the dish that was the centerpiece of the event. ("That made it real simple—you knew what you were coming to.")

The men tossed into the *sauce piquante* pot "something that they had killed hunting, either wild rabbit or wild duck, or a dove or quail, or turtle, and a lot of wild animals, like coon or squirrel. They'd just cook that any way they could. Usually it would be a red, tomato gravy, and real hot and spicy, so you could drink a lot of beer."

Terrance Simien's Pine Bark Stew

This spicy fish stew is widely known in Georgia and the Carolinas. There are several theories on where the name comes from. One is that the stew was often made outdoors over a fire of pine bark. The other is that the tender roots of the pine tree were used as a seasoning ingredient back during the eighteenth century.

5 slices bacon, cut in 1-inch pieces
2 cups diced potatoes
1 1/2 cups chopped onion
4 cups hot water
4 pounds whole freshwater fish (such as bass, perch, trout or bream), pan dressed, or 2 pounds fish filets

Salt and pepper
1 pound chopped fresh or 16 ounces canned tomatoes
1 1/2 tablespoons TABASCO® brand pepper sauce
1 tablespoon fresh thyme leaves, or 1 teaspoon dried

In a large, heavy pot, cook bacon over medium heat until crisp. Add potatoes and onion and cook 5 minutes or until onion is tender. Add water and bring to a boil. Season fish with salt and pepper and place in pot; reduce heat and simmer 10 minutes. Add remaining ingredients, simmer an additional 5 to 10 minutes or until fish flakes easily. Makes 6 servings.

Buddy Guy

Red-hot guitarist Buddy Guy commands his kitchen with the same indomitable authority that he shows on his Stratocaster.

"I got two things, my cookin' and guitar playin'," says Buddy. "When I come home off the road, I stop on the way home from the airport at the grocery store and get me whatever my mind's on. My wife can't stop me from going to the kitchen. She's a mom and dad to our kids when I'm gone, so I come in and tell her 'lay down on the couch and wait 'til the aroma hits you.' "

Buddy's love for sharing his cooking stems from childhood hours watching his mother around the stove. "I learned everything from my mom, but cooking is like playing guitar—you play like the people you learn a lot from, but something of your own gonna pop up in it."

For Guy, that translates into a lot of heat in his cooking. "I keep two bottles of Tabasco sauce in my bag with me at all times. That way even if I'm havin' chicken noodle soup or beef barley on the road, I can still get that Louisiana flavor."

In 1957, Guy tore himself away from Louisiana's cooking and the Baton Rouge blues clubs and migrated to Chicago. Club dates and food were scarce in the Windy City, and after six months Guy was spending days at a stretch going hungry. His luck finally changed after an impromptu stage challenge with Otis Rush, and Guy left the gig that night with a contract, finding Muddy Waters waiting outside for him with a salami sandwich and some kind words. Buddy wound up backing the Hoochie Coochie Man and Howlin' Wolf, as well as cutting his own sides for Chess Records.

Although he established himself as the musician's bluesman, Buddy's career stayed tepid as befuddled record companies couldn't figure out what to do with all Guy's high- voltage energy. In 1991, the retroactive recognition kicked in with a roar, as *Damn Right I've Got The Blues* found a revitalized Buddy schooling some of his most famous students, including Eric Clapton and Jeff Beck.

Since then, he's become a highly sought-after performer, ruling festival and club stages with equal dexterity. He runs his own club in Chicago, Buddy Guy's Legends, and if you're lucky you can catch him on a night when he's playing *and* cooking. When he's dishing out one of his high-octane solos or this Seafood Okra Gumbo, Buddy Guy knows you'll be back for second helpings.

Buddy Guy's Seafood Okra Gumbo

1/4 cup vegetable oil
1 large onion, chopped
1 bell pepper, chopped
1 pound sliced okra
2 cups chopped tomatoes
1 tablespoon minced garlic
About 3 cups shrimp stock
  (or fish stock from bouillon)
2 teaspoons Cajun or Creole
  seasoning
1 teaspoon salt
1 pound peeled and deveined
  medium shrimp
1/2 pound crabmeat
1/4 cup chopped fresh parsley
1 tablespoon TABASCO® brand
  pepper sauce
Hot cooked rice

Heat oil in a dutch oven or large cast
iron skillet over medium high heat.
Add onion, bell pepper and okra;
cook 5 minutes, stirring often.
Add tomatoes, garlic, stock, Cajun
seasonings and salt. Bring to a boil;
reduce heat to simmer and cook 30
minutes, stirring occasionally.
Stir in shrimp, crabmeat, parsley
and TABASCO sauce.
Cook 5 minutes longer or until
shrimp are done. Add additional
stock if gumbo is too thick.
Serve over rice.
Makes 6 servings.

Maria Muldaur

Maria Muldaur comes from a family of Sicilian cooks, but Hoppin' John—a traditional Southern New Year's Day dish—not pasta, has been the food that has fueled some of her landmark rock 'n' roll parties.

"For a good 20 years, I've been having huge New Year's Day parties, where people come after they've already partied to excess the night before," she says.

"I've had some famous parties and served this food. I had a couple at Woodstock back in the early '70s with The Band and Delaney and Bonnie Bramlett and Kris Kristofferson and just all kinds of people, a cast of thousands, and we just made vats of this stuff all day and served the appropriate cocktails as well."

"Then when I lived in Mill Valley (California), when I was in the Jerry Garcia Band, we'd have just hordes of people—Grateful Dead people with the attendant Hell's Angels. I've got pictures and memories of some great parties that have been based around this little menu. "So I've kind of taken this tradition with me wherever I go. Of course, it's well known in the South, but everybody loves it and calls up every year, 'Are you going to have your Hoppin' John party?' It's considered good luck to have these foods."

Maria's career has seen its share of good luck. Best known for her 1974 smash "Midnight At the Oasis," Maria has released a string of records that explored the jazz, blues and gospel genres, and appeared in several musicals. She re-emerged in 1992 with *Louisiana Love Call*, a tasty collection of "bluesiana" music that teamed her with numerous Louisiana legends, including Dr. John, Zachary Richard and several Neville brothers.

Though she has strayed from the culinary tradition of her ancestors, she still adds a Sicilian touch: "You put twice as many spices as it calls for, twice as much meat, a lot of lagniappe. When you're Sicilian, you never let well enough alone, in cooking or decorating or singing—you always have that extra lagniappe," she laughs.

One such bit of lagniappe is Tabasco sauce. "You throw some in there, but then you have several bottles on the table—not everybody is as spice-oriented as I am. That's the beauty of Tabasco—add spice at will."

Maria likes to swim laps in the afternoon, when her mind is turning toward dinner. Ideas for many of her culinary creations are hatched in the pool. "I'll think, 'OK, what's in the fridge? Let's see, I've got two chicken legs and a pepper.' I just invent really great, creative recipes that are easy to make."

"My recipes, if you put a spoonful of something as opposed to a half a spoonful, it doesn't much matter. They're not high-tech recipes—they're good, earthy recipes that are good to feed to hungry people. I hate fussy little recipes."

"Just like I am with my music, my cooking is improvisational, never the same twice, and full of passion and spice. Put plenty of the good stuff in it, and do it with all your heart and soul. And don't worry about mistakes, because they can turn into happy little creative accidents. "And," she adds with a laugh, "you can always fix it in the mix."

Maria Muldaur's Hoppin' John

"Hoppin' John" New Year's Day Good Luck Dinner

1 pound bag of dried black-eyed peas
   or several bags of frozen black-eyed peas
3 large meaty ham hocks
1 pound bacon, cut into 1-inch pieces
2 large yellow onions, chopped
2 stalks of celery, chopped very fine (include leaves)
1 teaspoon onion powder
1 1/2 teaspoons garlic powder
1 tablespoon dried thyme leaves, crushed
1 tablespoon TABASCO® brand pepper sauce
1/4 teaspoon black pepper
1 teaspoon salt (Janie's Crazy Mixed Up Salt if you can find it)

If using dried black-eyed peas, soak overnight according to package directions; drain.

Fill a separate large pot with water and start boiling smoked ham hocks for at least 45 minutes. In a large heavy kettle or Dutch oven, slowly cook bacon until it renders its fat, but don't let it get crisp. Add chopped onion and chopped celery until soft. Add pre-soaked black-eyed peas (or thawed frozen) and 2 cups of water (starting with the ham hock water) and adding more water if necessary.

When black-eyed peas come to a boil, reduce heat to medium; add ham hocks, seasonings and generous amounts of TABASCO sauce, at least 4-5 good shakes! Taste before adding pepper and salt (as bacon and ham hocks already provide some). Cook slowly, stirring to prevent sticking, and adding water as needed.

Add at least one more round of seasonings as the beans soak (they absorb the flavors). Maria Muldaur's cooking secret: The more onion powder you add, the more flavorful the beans become without adding more salt. When black-eyed peas are done, serve along with the following dishes:

• White boiled rice cooked according to package directions.
• Squares of fresh baked cornbread according to package directions (I add shredded cheddar cheese and a tiny bit of thinly chopped jalapeño peppers to batter before baking cornbread.)

Have TABASCO sauce on the table, so people can add as much as they prefer.

Good Ol' Southern Greens

3 good and meaty ham hocks
1 pound bacon, cut into 1-inch pieces
1 medium onion, coarsely chopped
3 cloves garlic, minced
4 one-pound bags of frozen collard greens, turnips, and/or mustard greens as suits you, plus a few bunches of fresh greens if you can find them
1 tablespoon salt
2 tablespoons cider vinegar
1 1/2 teaspoons onion powder
1 1/2 teaspoons garlic powder
3/4 teaspoon black pepper
1 tablespoon TABASCO® brand pepper sauce

Boil ham hocks in water for about 45 minutes.
In a large deep pot, add 1 pound of bacon and cook over medium heat until fat is rendered. Add onion and garlic; cook until soft.

In pot with ham hocks, cook frozen greens according to package directions, using ham hock water. Add onion and bacon (if ham hocks don't appeal to you, use cubed ham — but hocks are the traditional way).

Add cider vinegar and seasonings, tasting before adding salt, as bacon and hocks have already provided some of the salt. Add several generous dashes of TABASCO sauce.

Cook greens until well done, but not too overcooked. (This is Southern cooking — it ain't about no "light stir-fry"— vegetables are cooked long enough to be soft and full of flavor.

Prepare a large bowl of very finely chopped white or yellow onions.

Set out the kettle of black-eyed peas, the bowl of rice, the cornbread squares and the pot of greens, ham hocks and all! In both the peas and greens, the ham hocks should be pretty well fallen apart so there are nice chunks for everybody.

Put butter on the table for the cornbread, and several bottles of TABASCO sauce.

Instruct guests to spoon a little rice on a plate, then a generous helping of black-eyed peas over that. (Sprinkle with a little bit of raw onion, if desired). Spoon greens on top of the black-eyed peas. Add the cornbread on the side and there you have it — the traditional meal eaten in the South every New Year's Day. Black-eyed peas are for health, greens symbolize wealth and the cornbread is for happiness and good fortune in the coming year.

I've been having a "Hoppin' John" Party every New Year's Day for many, many years, and people love it. It is also a great cure for any of those darn pesky hangovers one just might wake up with after a wild night of New Year's partying.

Love, Maria

Irma Thomas

Photo: © Michael P. Smith

Irma Thomas, Soul Queen of New Orleans, Grammy Award winner, wife and mom, loves to cook. And cook she can.

Her red beans and rice carry a near-legendary status in the Crescent City, and she points out that "I also do a version of macaroni and cheese that is mouth-watering." She adds, "I like to be adventurous with my cooking. I make it up as I go...a pinch of this, a pinch of that. I always expand on recipes I've done before. I don't have as much time to cook as I would like, so when I get in the kitchen, look out."

Ms. Thomas has traveled widely and has sampled cooking from all over the world. "I consider myself a Southern cook as opposed to just a New Orleans or Louisiana cook. I use a lot of spices and condiments not usually found in food up North or in the East or West. We Southerners like our foods spicy. One of my favorite spices is Tabasco sauce. In fact, I had the privilege of performing for Mr. McIlhenny (the owner of McIlhenny Company, makers of Tabasco sauce) once. I used to carry a little bottle of it when I toured, but now it's available all over the country so I don't have to. That must come from people traveling to Louisiana and finding out how much we love our hot sauce."

The New Orleans Jazz and Heritage Festival, at which Ms. Thomas performs every year, is probably the best and biggest food and music extravaganza in the country. One of the most popular food items is crawfish bread.

"It's a great recipe," Irma says. "Jazz Fest is a perfect example of how food and music go together. They're both gratifying. Music can be very relaxing, and to some folks like myself, food is the same. To sit down and relax with a plate of your favorite food is like sitting down and listening to your favorite songs. You just kind of wiggle your toes, sit back and enjoy."

Irma Thomas has toured the world and performed with the likes of Bonnie Raitt and Dolly Parton, and recorded a duet with B.B. King. She performs often for charities and has sung the National Anthem for numerous events, including New Orleans Saints games. She sings in her church choir and is finally realizing a life-long dream: recording an all gospel album.

A deeply religious woman, Ms. Thomas adamantly states, "I don't sing gospel songs in my show because I don't want to give mixed messages. I know we're supposed to make a joyful noise, but I don't think finger poppin' and shakin' your booty to sacred songs is exactly what He was after. This album is my way of saying thank you in the biggest way for the voice that's been given to me.

"I have a simple philosophy. Stay optimistic—it's less stressful. Enjoy good friends, good music and good food."

Irma Thomas'
Stuffed Crawfish Bread

This is a popular snack at the New Orleans Jazz & Heritage Festival. If you can't get crawfish, you can substitute shrimp.

1/4 cup butter or margarine
2 cups chopped onion
1 cup chopped bell pepper
1 large clove garlic, minced
1 pound bag peeled crawfish tails (or shrimp)
1/3 cup chopped green onion
2 tablespoons TABASCO® brand pepper sauce
1 teaspoon salt
1/4 teaspoon black pepper

1 (48-ounce) package frozen bread dough
   (3 one-pound loaves), thawed
1 cup shredded mozzarella cheese
1 cup shredded cheddar cheese
Melted butter or margarine

Melt 1/4 cup butter or margarine in a large skillet (not iron) over medium heat. Add onion and cook 5 minutes or until onion is very tender. Stir in bell pepper and garlic and cook 5 to 10 minutes longer or until peppers are tender. Add crawfish, green onion, TABASCO sauce, salt and pepper, mixing well. Cover and simmer 5 minutes. Remove from heat and set aside.

Preheat oven to 350° F. One loaf at a time, roll out bread dough on a lightly floured surface to about a 20x5-inch rectangle and cut into 4 pieces, each about 5x5 inches. Spoon about 1/4 cup crawfish mixture in center of each piece and top with about 1 tablespoon of each cheese. Moisten edges of dough with a little water and fold dough over, pinching edges to seal. Shape gently with hands into 5-inch loaves. Place on greased baking sheet and brush with melted butter.
Bake for 25 to 30 minutes or until golden brown. Remove from oven and brush again with melted butter. Serve warm. Makes 12 servings.

It was during a visit with Paul McIlhenny at the TABASCO® factory, surrounded by the tropical beauty of Avery Island, that we first talked about this cookbook. That's when we discovered that, along with a taste for good food, we shared the same opinion about real music.

Yes, real music — the kind of music that the people featured in this book play: the blues, rhythm and blues, gospel, jazz, zydeco and roots-based rock & roll. The kind of music that you'll hear from the electric fingers of Buddy Guy, the bayou blasts of Buckwheat Zydeco's accordion and the royal voice of New Orleans' own Soul Queen Irma Thomas.

My own love for these sounds dates back to my childhood in Jackson, Tennessee. We got our culture at night in Jackson — 50,000 watts of it, coming over two stations on the AM radio. At one end of the dial were the classic blues and soul then being recorded for the Stax and Chess labels, and on the other were the plaintive strings of some of the finest country music of the day. I knew then that I had to get to Beale Street in Memphis; and by the time I was 17, I was working as a driver for Bukka White and Furry Lewis.

This music was still ringing in my ears in 1992 when I founded the first House of Blues in Cambridge, Massachusetts. For me, the most exciting aspect of the House of Blues has been the nonprofit House of Blues Foundation. With a board of directors that includes many of the finest blues scholars in the world, the House of Blues Foundation seeks to promote racial harmony by teaching the social, spiritual and artistic legacy of the blues. We do this by sending artists into schools, sponsoring music scholarships and, during the day, turning the House of Blues nightclub itself into a learning laboratory for area students.

What does the blues have to teach us? If you ever join a daytime House of Blues tour, you will learn that, for these kids, the blues has a lot to say. First of all, the music gets their attention. Accompanied by a blues guitarist who demonstrates the music from each period of history, our tour takes students back to Africa,

through the middle passage and onto the American continent. They learn (many of them for the first time) about the brutal efforts to strip Africans of their gods, their clothes and their culture. And it's the blues — always the blues — that teaches them how the total effort eventually failed.

The African roots and the American adaptations of the blues are a living testament to the enduring strength of the people who play and sing the music. That's why the House of Blues has become the most requested field trip in the Boston area.

It is especially exciting to be establishing the Louisiana chapter of the House of Blues Foundation, which will be linked to the New Orleans House of Blues. New Orleans is, after all, a cultural capital of the world and the life force of some of the world's greatest music. It's also gratifying that a portion of the proceeds from this cookbook are earmarked for this Louisiana chapter.

Thanks, Paul. And that Josh White gospel tape that I promised you is on its way.

IN BLUES WE TRUST

Isaac B. Tigrett